STEAM
ENTERTAINMENT

YE RAILWAY STATION DURING YE HOLIDAY
TIME IN YE ROMAN PERIOD

(From a rare old frieze (not) in ye British Museum)

186

STEAM
ENTERTAINMENT

JOHN R. HUME
and
BARON F. DUCKHAM

DAVID & CHARLES
NEWTON ABBOT LONDON
NORTH POMFRET (VT) VANCOUVER

0 7153 6645 9

Set in 10/11pt Monotype Garamond
by Avontype (Bristol) Limited
and printed in Great Britain
by Biddles Limited   Guildford   Surrey
for David & Charles (Holdings) Limited
South Devon House   Newton Abbot   Devon

Published in the United States of America
by David & Charles Inc   North Pomfret
Vermont 05053   USA

Published in Canada by Douglas David &
Charles Limited   3645 McKechnie Drive
West Vancouver BC

Contents

Introduction

The age of steam lasted for some 250 years. Newcomen's engine, first recorded at Dudley in 1712, is the recognised ancestor of all reciprocating steam engines. During the next century steam became common in mining, metal working, cotton spinning and brewing. By the 1800s it was beginning to make its appearance in the realm of transport. Whatever entertainment value possessed by these early machines was purely adventitious and largely unrecorded. Smeaton went as a boy to observe the erection of a Newcomen engine near his home and George Stephenson, too, showed a youthful interest in the pumping and winding engines of the colleries around his birthplace.

It was however the application of steam to transport that introduced the steam engine to an ever wider public. Symington's early experiment with Patrick Miller on a Dumfriesshire loch with a small paddle steamer had the poet Robert Burns as an interested spectator. More explicitly entertaining was the exhibition in London of Trevithick's locomotive *Catch Me, Who Can?* in 1808.

The hard commercialism of the railway age was softened by the appeal of steam. Large crowds attended the opening of new lines from the Stockton & Darlington Railway (1825) onwards and almost every extension of the railway network was opened in carnival spirit. Needless to say the locomotive was the centre of attraction, particularly when bright, seductive liveries and polished metalwork appeared to dazzle the passenger. Generations of boys found a new hobby in train watching and even grown men might flock to see the departure of expresses. Even though for the seasoned – and sometimes sorely tried – traveller the glamour of railways often wore a little thin, the discomforts were seldom held against the steam locomotive.

Much of the appeal of the locomotive was shared by the steamship, particularly by the paddle steamer, whose exposed engines with their flashing brightwork, gave a daunting impression of power. Many such steamers were built expressly for pleasure outings and were often gaily decorated. Indeed the mass entertainment of the Victorians came to be heavily dependent on both steamer and rail excursions. At a more personal level the wealthy built steam yachts for ocean cruising and launches provided for private pleasure on lake and river.

Fairs completed their transition from markets to amusement centres with the introduction of steam-powered roundabouts, swings and organs. Showmen vied with each other to produce novelty, while their use of traction engines for haulage and power gave pleasure to many. The relatively manageable size of fairground and similar engines has made them attractive to preservationists in recent years.

The desire to own a steam engine – or a whole railway – was catered for by miniaturisation. The larger scale miniature railways reflected the affluence of the upper class enthusiast, but nowadays the pleasure of the few has become the entertainment of the many: several notable country estates run such lines today for their visitors. With the disappearance of steam from our railways nostalgia helped to motivate 'preservation' groups who sought to recapture some of the atmosphere of the age of steam. By their efforts they have in fact created a new form of steam entertainment.

In these pages we have tried to suggest something of the rich variety of experience that steam has provided. The almost living quality of the steam engine has earned for it a unique place in man's affection.

Steamers and Launches

Like steam railways, steamships were originally designed for utility. Any 'entertainment value' they possessed was entirely adventitious and eagerly seized upon by the merciless caricaturists of Regency or early Victorian Britain. But well before the day of the railway excursion, the steamboat had already been pressed into service on Britain's estuaries to provide pleasure trips as well as regular (at first somewhat irregular!) services. Within only a year or two of Henry Bell's *Comet* (1812) the smoky, puffing paddle steamer was arousing the ire of many a sailing sloop's master on our greater rivers. It was no consolation to plead the admitted precedence of sail over steam after being rammed by some clanking 'floating kettle' whose speed you had misjudged.

Early voyagers, too, often enough found little entertainment. Thames steamers were for a time notorious for the number of passengers they drowned, while on the Yorkshire Ouse the hapless traveller was required to help refloat a grounded vessel. Sir George Head, writing in 1836, described how the captain of a Selby–Hull steamer made his forty-odd passengers run 'like sheep at the bark of a dog' from one side of the deck to the other at the gruff command 'rowl her'. Yet despite the delays of tide or engine failure and the perils of boiler explosion the steamer of the pre-railway age was well patronised. Apart from contributing to London's urban transport, Thames steamboats permitted city 'gents' – like that admirable sporting grocer Mr Jorrocks with his hamper of 'weal, half a ham, beef, sarsingers, chickens, sherry white and all that sort of thing' – to make a fun-filled trip to the flesh-pots of Margate and back.

The coming of the railways killed off some of the regular river services, though often only after a bitter struggle. Pleasure runs remained; indeed where railway companies bought their way into steamer operation, co-ordinated rail and water excursions became possible. On the scenic Firth of Clyde a veritable golden age of steam was by the late nineteenth century allowing the teeming population of Glasgow to experience all the delights of a trip 'doon the watter' – strong refreshments and all. River, loch, and coastal resort especially all boasted their steamers, catering mainly perhaps for the vast armies of the lower middle class and 'respectable' artisans. The very rich might have their private steam yachts whose sleek white hulls and rakish rig were equally at home in the Channel or cruising off the Cote d'Azur.

In the twentieth century the decline of the pleasure steamer and launch has been – in Britain at least – even more nearly complete than that of the steam railway. Active railway preservation societies have salvaged for future generations all the essentials of the steam rail journey. But, with only a very few exceptions, the steamer is now a thing of the past, while even motor vessel services dedicated to pure entertainment are less than abundant.

When today the British take to the water hell-bent on pleasure, it is in a sailing dinghy or on water skis.

The earliest British steamboats were undoubtedly those associated with the names of three Scotsmen: Patrick Miller, a retired merchant and banker, James Taylor, tutor to Miller's family, and the famous engineer William Symington. Although Miller had steamed a crude vessel (the *Edinburgh*) on the Forth in 1787, it was only after Taylor had brought Miller and Symington together that real success was achieved. The maiden voyage of Symington's tiny steamboat took place on a small loch on Miller's estate at Dalswinton, Dumfriesshire on 14 October 1788. Though Symington lost Miller's patronage and was due for further frustrations in his later work, the initial voyage, pictured above, at least gave 'great pleasure' to the wondering spectators of Dalswinton. It was the seed of steam-based entertainment on Scottish waters.

(*Above*) Symington's most famous vessel, the ill-fated *Charlotte Dundas* (pictured here), was to give permanent pleasure to no one. Named after the daughter of Lord Dundas (a director of the Forth & Clyde Canal), the boat possessed a single rear paddle wheel and was intended to introduce steam towage to this well-known Scottish navigation. Despite the impressive trials of March 1802 – which at first inspired the directors to order eight such tugs – the erosion of the canal sides by the steamer's wash brought disillusionment. The orders were cancelled and the *Charlotte Dundas* was left to go derelict.

(*Below*) Henry Bell's *Comet* of 1812, however, firmly renewed Scotland's place in the history of steam navigation at a time when the initiative appeared to be crossing to America. Moreover its inaugural voyage from John Wood's yard at Port Glasgow up to Glasgow on 6 August 1812 may be said to have in essence begun the great era of Clyde steamers. Regular services soon were in hand between the Broomielaw, Greenock and the newly laid out and highly fashionable Helensburgh. They were the earliest timetabled, commercial steaming in Europe and were soon imitated on other great rivers such as the Thames, the Mersey and the Yorkshire Ouse-Humber. Though some scoffed at such 'singing kettles', most sources assure us that the public was only too anxious to sample the delights (and trials!) of the panting river steamers.

The 150th anniversary of Bell's *Comet* was too good an occasion to miss. Since the original had been built on the site of what by 1962 was Lithgow's East Yard, it was appropriate that Lithgows should fit out the replica. Local firms helped in cash and kind and much careful research was done to ensure accuracy. (Fortunately the original engine is preserved at the Science Museum, South Kensington). The replica had a fine ceremonial launching at Port Glasgow and then sailed across the Clyde to Helensburgh with a distinguished company on board, all suitably attired in the costume of the time. And after this imaginative and rewarding piece of steam entertainment, a wreath was laid on Henry Bell's tomb at Rhu. Our plates show the launch and the voyage of 1 September 1962 to Helensburgh.

The bustle of Glasgow's Broomielaw in its hey-day has been famed in song and legend. No British river could compete with the Firth of Clyde in its scenic and unashamedly romantic appeal – and the Broomielaw was the natural point of embarkation. The beauties of Rothesay and the Kyles of Bute might often be appreciated through a grey estuarine mist (or just an honest alcoholic haze), but here was cheap mass entertainment, warm-hearted and gregarious. Our photograph dates from 1895 and if you hadn't the price of a fare there was still plenty of shipping activity and human spectacle to observe and enjoy.

Glasgow was of course not the only port where the golden age of the Clyde steamer could be enjoyed.

Above is the *Neptune*, a Glasgow & South Western Railway steamer built in 1892, entering Ayr harbour. The *Neptune* did a great deal of summer excursion work, prided herself on being faster than her Caledonian Railway competitors of similar vintage and was a popular vessel in her day. Much more interesting than Ayr (for the steam paddleboat enthusiast) was Rothesay, here prictured below around the turn of the century, probably rather before 1900. Rothesay was – and indeed remains – a veritable jewel of the lower Clyde (to use travel agents' journalese) and was a natural goal for many a tired Clydesider. The vessels depicted are the *Benmore* (foreground) and the *Mercury*, sister ship of the *Neptune* and launched in the same year.

(*Above*)

Entertainment is an ambiguous concept. This rare deck photograph of the 1890s on the Clyde steamer *Mercury* records little if any open fun. Certainly the elderly lady in the right foreground scarcely appears to have been making a pleasure voyage. But the blacks and whites of the plate should not make us assume a funereal gloom was prevailing. The picture speaks of expectation; though whether of arrival or departure is not entirely clear.

(*Opposite page*)

Like other forms of steam propulsion the paddle boat is now very nearly a thing of the past. Not before time societies are being founded to preserve something of this fascinating mechanical heritage. The two illustrations show a very special vessel indeed: *Waverley* (IV). Launched in 1946 to help make up wartime losses, she was built for the then London & North Eastern Railway – a direct successor in name and traditions to the earlier ships of the North British Railway's fleet. *Waverley* could carry over 1,300 passengers and in her twenty-odd years of operation gave pleasure to countless thousands more. She was to become the last Clyde paddle steamer. Here she is, pictured in the 1960s, first at Rothesay (probably preparing for a Bute cruise) and then at Gourock pier.

(*Above*) Steam on the Thames (rather than 'London River') could never rival the Clyde. Yet it had its own magic and, when associated with events such as the Henley Regatta or with late Victorian and Edwardian memories of those (allegedly) endless summer Sundays at Maidenhead, it assumes a subtle aura of elitism. Could any small vessel look finer than the steam yacht *Emily*, dressed overall at Henley in c1873?

(*Above, opposite page*) The Thames Cup at Henley was scarcely a steam occasion, but nowadays only the keenest oarsman would fail to thrill to the tiny steam boat *Loddon*. Assuredly it would be more fun to operate than the other craft pictured here on a perfect summer's day of c1885.

(*Below, opposite page*) And while we speak of summer, perhaps a closer peep at the distinguished Henley spectators is permissible, even if steam is not in evidence. This group was photographed in c1895. (They must have reached Henley by steam; many of them, anyhow!)

Any reference to steam on the Thames is automatically a reference to the Salter Brothers of Oxford. Their cheerful steamers, slipping quietly by with a wisp of smoke and a dignified chug, were always a beautiful part of the river scene. (*Below*) is *Cliveden*, built by Salters in 1931 and converted to diesel in 1966. The *Majestic* (*above*) was an older vessel, built and used by Cawston's of Reading as a pleasure boat. Launched in 1908, she was acquired by Salters in the 1930s and indeed proved to be their last steamboat. This photograph was taken on 5 August 1966, the year she was withdrawn from service. It might be mentioned that not everyone along the Thames welcomed steam unreservedly. In 1884 Sir Gilbert Augustus Clayton East, Bart, stated that although he liked to see the respectable working classes enjoying themselves on the river, he objected strongly to the 'real river roughs [who] offend by their appearance, their language and their deeds'. Yet he felt the steam launches preferable to the rowing boats since the former 'pass by and are gone'. Elitism died hard.

Over the years a bewildering variety of steamers plied the waters of the Thames. Here is the *Donola*, built in 1893 at Teddington as the *Lodona* apparently for one of the partners in Huntley & Palmer, the famous biscuit firm. She has a steel hull and an overall length of 58ft. She was subsequently owned by the Thames Conservancy (as an inspection launch) which presented her to the National Maritime Museum in 1969. By contrast, the little wooden-hulled *Janet* was apparently built at Leigh-on-Sea in 1950. She was later fitted out with a steam engine (built in 1961) and as can be seen right has become a 'tidy little boat' in which some distinguished steam enthusiasts have sailed.

It has been emphasised that all greater (and several lesser) rivers had their pleasure steamers. Lack of space prevents a fair geographic coverage; so let the Trent serve as an example of the many. Nottingham's Trent Bridge was presumably always a popular venue for a stroll and an obliging city corporation even provided a 'Lovers' Walk' in 1873 running upstream on the southern bank. A little later private enterprise (J. H. Witty) started steamer services between Trent Bridge and Colwick Park. The *Sunbeam* made her maiden trip in 1886 and was joined two years later by the *Queen*. Witty introduced a third boat, the *Empress* in 1896 and by that year was able to run a 27min summer service every day of the week. During the golden years of these steamers passengers were regaled with music *en route* on each vessel. Our plate above shows the *Empress* warping into her berth while the *Sunbeam* prepares to leave for Colwick Park with a full complement of passengers. The year is 1898.

During the nineteenth century an enormous number of small steam launches were built to pamper the life of a rich boating enthusiast or to make more pleasurable the periodic inspection of canal or river navigation by a group of trustees. (*Opposite page*) Top right is the *Bernardino de Campos*, possibly preparing for a trial run after being launched in 1896 by Cochran & Co of Birkenhead. She is in every way typical of the small steam craft of the period intended for the kind of use on river or lake which we have outlined. A survivor of an even earlier era is seen (*below*) right. This photograph of the *Ullswater* sailing on Lake Windermere was taken in June 1967 during the summer meeting of the Newcomen Society. Originally built somewhere between 1850 and 1860 she subsequently sank in Ullswater and remained submerged for about seventy-five years. This beautifully restored vessel – with original boiler and engine be it added – belongs to Mr George Pattinson of Windermere.

(*Above*)
Much grander steam yachts were fairly commonly owned by members of the nobility (and of course royalty) who had a nautical turn of mind. This smart vessel, the *Cleopatra*, was built for Il Hami Pacha, son of a sometime Viceroy of Egypt.

(*Above, opposite page*)
A later vessel of the same ilk was the handsome twin-screw steam yacht *Dolaura*, constructed around 1900 to the order of the Hon James Dunsmure of Victoria BC. Here she makes a fine sight during her trials on the Clyde. Yachts such as these could undertake extensive sea voyages, though doubtless in most cases they haunted the fashionable resorts of the Mediterranean or the Aegean islands. This particular vessel could make a comfortable twelve knots, but who would want to hurry the voyage on such a smart ship?

(*Below, opposite page*)
More democratic, if a trifle less elegant, were the pleasure steamers of the sea-side resorts. We have already noted those of the Clyde – but here regular services and pleasure trips overlapped and the vessels were a superior race apart. But for a few hours or so around the bay (perhaps daringly out of sight of land) thousands of summer holiday-makers turned to the local steamer at the pier – whether it was Scarborough, Margate, or wherever. One of the most celebrated was the much-loved *Brighton Queen*, here crowded with a full complement of passengers. Everything clearly depended on the weather; but come sun or squall so tightly packed a voyage would always rate as 'an experience'. The *Brighton Queen* was owned by P. & A. Campbell and usually ran from Brighton to Eastbourne and Hastings, and sometimes across the Channel.

(*Above*)

A popular ship on the Bristol Avon and Severn Estuary was the *Lady Margaret*, introduced in 1895 by Edwards & Robertson, but purchased by P. & A. Campbell the following year. She was apparently used for the Bristol to Weston-super-Mare run, but finished her days as an Admiralty tender. Our photograph cannot be later than 1903, for the *Lady Margaret* was sold out of the Campbell fleet in that year. Here the Avon Gorge affords a magnificent back-cloth to this fine vessel.

(*Opposite page*)

Last, but assuredly not least, in our pageant of water-borne steam is the *Maid of the Loch*, known to every Glaswegian and every visitor to Scotland's most celebrated Loch. She is the biggest (as she is also the last) of Loch Lomond steamers and came into service as late as May 1953. She presumably owed her paddles to the need to negotiate shallows at Luss, though ironically Luss pier was closed shortly after she was ordered! Aesthetically the *Maid of the Loch* is one of the minor successes of transport nationalisation, though financial losses on the service have sometimes been considerable. Our views are of her leaving Tarbet during the 1972 season.

Did we say last? Well, fortunately with steam the end never does come, at least not to the true initiate. This young enthusiast viewing superb models of the *Jupiter* and *Maid of Argyll* is blissfully unaware of the economics of steam entertainment. Maxwell Park, Glasgow, has become for him the Clyde of yesteryear where her steamers still prepare to provide their unique pleasure.

Fairgrounds and Traction Engines

'All the fun of the fair' is a dictum which predates the age of steam. Fairs, as great periodic markets, go back to ancient times. Held throughout Christendom on and around saints' days, they quite early provided a variety of entertainments as fringe activities to their mercantile function. Improved communications and more sophisticated trading patterns gradually eroded the economic importance of most fairs during the eighteenth and nineteenth centuries. Yet the popular need for mass enjoyment was heightened by the drabness of industrialisation; and to the traditional gipsy's booth or travelling stage were added the mechanical pleasures of the roundabout. Steam made its contribution both as a means of power and as a considerable aid to transport for itinerant shows and amusements.

To William Bray of Folkestone belongs the distinction of providing the world with its first showman's engine: in August 1859 one of his engines was billed by Myer's 'Great American Circus' to pull 'the Magnificent Band Carriage' which preceded a grand procession of performers and animals. By the 1870s Sidney Soame was using a small portable steam engine to drive a roundabout in Norfolk. He and Frederick Savage, who had founded an engine-building business at King's Lynn, appear to have collaborated for a time and before long Savage was an honoured name among those who supplied small engines for fairgrounds. Soon steam was helping to entertain millions by powering gaily coloured roundabouts, swings and even jauntily-toned organs. But for many a visitor to the fair, the supreme glory was the showman's engine itself. Magnificent examples by Fowlers, Marshalls, Burrells and others proved to be perennial show stealers. A makers' catalogue of 1906 speaks proudly of their engines being 'tastefully decorated with twisted brass columns supporting the roof; stars, rings or other ornaments . . . and finished in an elaborate style'.* Whether driving electric generators or simply hauling heavy fairground equipment, the showman's engine was the recognised prince of steam road vehicles.

Happily many of the whole gamut of steam vehicles – from fairground engine to the more prosaic though still beautiful steam tractor or road roller – have been lovingly preserved. And for the steam enthusiast the frequently held traction engine rallies nowadays more than compensate for the absence of steam from the few remaining fairs. Only thirteen engines participated in the first organised rally, held at Appleford, Oxfordshire on 6 June 1953. Today few areas are without a regular traction engine rally; and some at least, with their steam yachts and 'glorious golden galloping horses' provide as much fun as any old time fair.

* Quoted by Philip Wright, *Traction Engines* (1959)

A wool fair and a strangers' market, with their own church of St Giles, were features of medieval Oxford. The fringe activities of fairs became more important as their economic role declined until by the nineteenth century the amusement aspect was often the only one left. Here, near the famous Martyrs' Memorial can be seen one of the earliest forms of steam roundabout: Ayer's 'steam dobbies'. It is about 1895 and a group of neatly dressed and well-shod children patiently await their turn to ride the bucking steam horses.

An age innocent of the cinema, television or even of much time for leisure activities valued highly the periodic opportunities for the pursuit of pleasure. Steam made possible a great deal of mechanically-based fun and fairs were well patronised by both middle and working classes. In this view below of St Giles', Oxford, around 1900, the variety of headware is as interesting as the entertainments provided. The steam-driven attractions included George Bird's galloping horses (which apparently came to St Giles' as early as 1870) and Collins' cake walk.

Rather more sophisticated machines were soon available to keep mechanical entertainment up to date. No industry is more conscious of the need to move with the times! New forms of motion might be offered, like this 'joy wheel' or 'razzle dazzle'. Here the seating revolved at a tilte'd angle while the whole structure rocked from side to side.

Another attempt at modernity was roundabouts with imitation motor-cars and an undulating motion. Such 'Motor Car Switchbacks', as they were known were a popular ride before 1914 and all the bigger showmen travelled at least one. Here many a young artisan must have experienced his first taste of the joys of motoring – a hobby which was then far beyond his modest pocket. Nowadays when motor cars have become a way of life (and death) one looks back somewhat wistfully at these 'pretend' cars and their reliance on steam.

But for sheer excitement has anything at the fair ever equalled the steam yacht? 'Shamrocks' there were in plenty, and older readers will well remember the intrepid young bloods and their girl friends (shrieking with a mixture of delight and horror) clinging for their lives as the 'racing yachts' produced a rapidity of motion unknown in the roughest sea. The protective netting bespoke the possible dangers as it also issued its challenge. These yachts were supplied by Savage in 1914 to those well known Bradford showmen, the Waddington brothers.

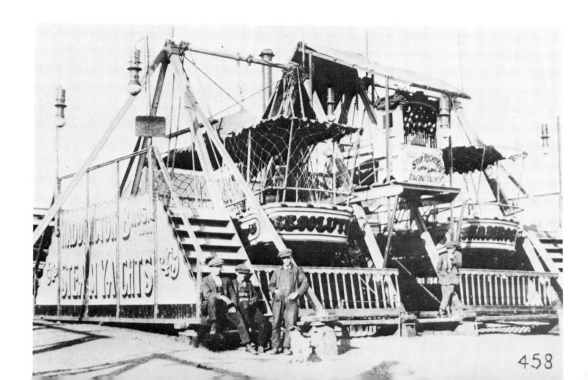

This precursor of the big wheel, also anxious to stress its role as 'a ride of the present day', was photographed at Hull fair in 1906. For a pre-decimal halfpenny you could have your heart in your mouth, attain a brief bird's eye view of the milling fairground and forget for a little while the harsher realities of everyday life. This particular 'ride' was known as Lieske's 'Steam Overcoats'.

Probably the only set of twin yachts still in existence which relies on steam power is this superb pair, pictured here at the Harewood House rally in 1970. The yachts were built by Frederick Savage of King's Lynn and were long operated by the famous showman Harry Lee. Interestingly, Lee married the daughter of Herbert Waddington who with his brother Walter owned the steam yachts shown in the previous plate. This set dates from 1900 or shortly afterwards.

Show business is traditionally connected with 'the bright lights'. In fact showmen were among the first to use electric lighting and power. To illuminate the hundreds of light bulbs on roundabouts or organs portable generators ('electric light engines') were used which could be drawn by traction engine or horse. The example shown (*below*) is by Savage of King's Lynn and was owned by James Hibbert, whose proprietor's plate describes him as 'Emperor of Showmen'. Certainly he travelled extensively in Lancashire and Cheshire.

Fairs without music would have been miserable affairs. From ancient times wandering musicians played to entertain the crowds and it was inevitable that steam should eventually be pressed into service to produce sounds 'to beguile the spirit'. (*Above*) the modern visitors to the 1970 Harewood House rally may not be exactly beguiled, but young and old show undoubted interest in this 98-key Gavioli organ, powered by steam. Many such organs once toured the country fairs. This one was presented by the Show Organ Preservation Society after careful restoration by Mr George Parmley of Durham.

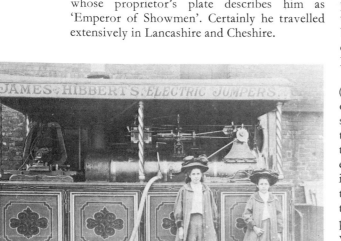

(*Above, opposite page*) From the late 1890s the development of the cinematograph added to the showman's stock-in-trade, gradually superseding the efforts of troups of travelling actors. Again the power chain led back to steam; and the early bioscope, together with the lighting of its theatre, ultimately relied on generators like that shown below or on others activated by traction engines. In the latter case, as in this picture taken at Darwen about 1905, the engine was thrown out of gear and a leather belt transmitted power from the fly wheel to the generator. Layland, the owner of this particular show later started a number of village cinemas in Yorkshire and Lancashire.

Transportation was necessarily a matter of the closest concern to showmen and a large proportion of their lives was spent either on the road or in setting up and later dismantling their equipment. Steam began to replace the horse from the late nineteenth century in the shape of some of the most beautiful traction engines ever built. They were, however, no luxury to showmen, but an absolute essential if heavy new roundabouts were to be dragged from one end of the country to the other.

Greens (*below*), claimed to tour 'all England' and, judging from the faces of the fairmen in the plate, have been caught here by the camera just before departure for yet another appointment with fun. Assuredly it was scarcely a life of fun for the itinerant labour force, though steam must in some measure have lightened their burden. The engine shown is *His Majesty*, built by Burrell, and photographed at Newton Abbot, probably in the late 1920s.

(*Above*)

'The morning service' springs to mind as a caption to this scene; certainly the camera appears to have intruded on an act of worship. But indeed those enthusiasts who have rescued, restored and taken on the maintenance of traction engines need both faith and devotion. All lovers of steam owe them an incalculable debt for their vision and perseverance. This magnificent showman's engine, fortunate in its immaculate restoration by its owner, Mr R. Preston of Potto, Yorkshire, was built in 1913 by Burrell for Emersons' of Cumberland as showman's loco 3526, *Lightning II*.

Traction engine rallies, as we have noted, have become one of the purest forms of steam entertainment. Their obvious attraction for large numbers of people and their need for abundant space have meant that they have often become part of today's stately homes syndrome. Woburn Abbey, Nostell Priory and Harewood House are just some of the venues of famous rallies.

(*Opposite page*) These two plates show what is universally acclaimed as one of the very best of such meetings: that held at Woburn Abbey under the patronage of the Duke of Bedford.

The gentleman in the white overall on the footplate of the little Burrell compound is the Duke himself, who appears to be steering with enviable skill.

One of the most important events at any rally is the grand parade. Here the engines can proceed in a stately manner before an admiring crowd. (And crowds can be very large, as the photograph shows). The grand parade often opens the afternoon's entertainment and provides an opportunity for an expert commentator to tell the crowd about the performance and history of each engine. The leading engine (*above*), Mr Arthur Napper's *Old Timer*, featured in a famous race for a firkin of beer in 1950 which started the whole rally movement.

Very much 'in steam', (*below*), at the Harewood House rally of 1970 is Marshall's number 47825, an admirable general purpose engine built in 1909. This model was bought and restored by the late Mr E. Meadowcroft of Crayke, Yorkshire, and is, we believe, still owned by the family.

Providing a backcloth to the engine in the previous plate is the 'olde tyme' steam fair. This general view, with the magnificent trees and squat tower of Harewood Church looking timelessly on, recaptures something of the fun and jollity of village entertainment a good half century or more ago. For older visitors it is sometimes an occasion for shameless nostalgia; youngsters simply enjoy all around them without too many thoughts about any 'world we have lost'.

At rallies the traction engine is rightly king. But other forms of steam locomotion give pleasure – as they gave it in the past. Here is a truly delightful steam wagon, *Pendle Queen*, built as number 940 in 1917 by the Yorkshire Patent Steam Wagon Company, Hunslet, Leeds. Bought in the nick of time from a scrapyard, it has been wonderfully restored by Mr T. Varley of Guisburn.

It is not merely at rallies, however, that the pleasures of steam road engines can be enjoyed. Enthusiastic owners need to keep their splendid vehicles in the prime of mechanical condition. Odd stretches of private estate or quiet country lanes provide a little exercise, too, between the mass events. For those who come across this restored Aveling steam roller, above, there is the joy of genuine rediscovery; for the engine and its occupants, many admiring or even envious glances. But how charmingly improbable that *two* steam rollers can still encounter each other!

In yet more sylvan settings the beauty and mystery of steam appear still more appropriate – though Wordsworth and Hardy assuredly would have disagreed. In an age of road juggernauts the slow motion and rhythmic sighs of this McLaren single-cylinder agricultural engine surely blend more pleasurably with the background than any internal combustion engine could. Possibly the 1911 Stanley steam car is a more doubtful intruder into the poet's Lakeland, though its sins (if any) are venial compared with the modern power boats on Windermere or the results of the motorway.

Catching them young is important in any field. Nowhere more so than in steam preservation where even the most junior pair of hands can be usefully employed. The youngster (*opposite page*) still seems somewhat bemused by the sheer array of steam power; and the proud owner may not yet be weighing up his admirer's work potential. But (*below*) the heart of one young man has been truly enraptured by the charm of steam, though one fears that the white shirt will not long remain proof against coal dust and oil. No matter.

The preservation of steam road vehicles, whether for show or purely private entertainment, is a matter of hard work. Of course it is a labour of love, but as has sometimes been observed, we would not undertake half the tasks of our leisure hours if it were a question of paid employment. (*Right*) Mr Jack Wakefield applies a little elbow grease to Burrell 3397, *Cock O' the North*, photographed at Newcastle-upon-Tyne in 1966.

Railways: the appeal of steam

Of all the applications of steam power, the railway locomotive holds the prime place in popular affection. In times past ordinary people, as well as railway enthusiasts, flocked to main line stations to see new or famous locomotives, and the crowds visiting preserved railways include many such, for whom the steam locomotive is both lovable and mysterious. The continuing appearance in the railway press of reminiscent articles is another aspect of the same feeling. It is not nostalgia – but something more vibrant. Many writers have tried to describe the attraction of the locomotive, and most stress its human characteristics – its noisiness, its messiness, its fallibility but at the same time its sometimes incredible beauty. And it is steam, blasting from the exhaust, shrilly escaping from the safety valves or from the cylinder cocks, or gently leaking from a joint or gland, that is the essence of its spell. Perhaps it is in the resemblance to women that the steam locomotive attracts so many men – its warmth, its moods, and the many faces of its loveliness. It is surely not surprising that great artists like Monet, Turner and Sisley drew inspiration from steam railways, and that the composer, Dvorak was passionately fond of locomotives. Men of God, dons, farmers, business men, and a host of others, articulate and inarticulate, have found pleasure in the steam locomotive: sometimes entertainment in its frothier sense, but often a rich, deep feeling of wonder and awe that a creation of man should seem so harmonious with nature. The quiet satisfaction of the branch line train, the sleek sophistication of the high-speed flier, the lonely odyssey of the highland train were all aspects of an experience, the more precious because it could be savoured so universally, and because it was an unsought for bonus to the business of travelling.

Wreathed in steam. Class A4 Pacific *Bittern* emerges from Springburn Road Bridge, St Rollox, Glasgow on a Glasgow-Aberdeen train in 1967. This service was the last regular A4 turn, and no fewer than three of the four A4s preserved in Britain ended their days on it, including *Bittern*.

There was almost always a small knot of spectators to see the departure of these A4-hauled trains from Glasgow.

Polluter *par excellence*. The grandest visual displays made by steam locomotives involved smoke as well as steam, and photographers have used all the tricks of their art to emphasise exhaust to aesthetic effect. Here a BR class 5MT 4–6–0 with Caprotti valve-gear produces enough grime to satisfy the most ardent steam enthusiast – and to antagonise the most lukewarm environmentalist.

(*Above*) Barclay beautified. The small industrial locomotive was scorned by many enthusiasts who preferred the more obvious glitter and glamour of main-line operation. For many people in industrial areas, however, the pug was a part of life. Even in surroundings that were basically squalid, beauty could sometimes be found. In a district dominated by pit bings, a Barclay 0–4–0ST (NCB Twechar area No 6) is seen crossing the Forth & Clyde Canal at Twechar with a train of empties in 1962.

(*Below*) Beetlecrusher at work! The dockside shunter, though not glamorous, was a much-loved feature of many ports. Standard designs by private locomotive-builders were common, but the larger dock owning railway companies usually had their own specialised designs. J. F. McIntosh's attractive 0–6–0T earned its insecticidal nickname by virtue of its heavy appearance.

Here one is seen at Queen's Dock, Glasgow, in 1960.

(*Above*) Steam and sunlight. The last days of steam in many areas were times of minimum maintenance, with leaking joints giving aesthetic appeal at the expense of operating efficiency. In this view a BR class 3 MT 2–6–0 steams gently at Kilmarnock in 1966.

(*Below*) Steam and snow. A class A3 Pacific passes Balornock, Glasgow in 1963, with wintry weather showing off the exhaust to advantage.

Steam the much-beloved. Locomotive wor-
shippers contemplating class A1 4–6–2 No 60145

on the last regular steam working at York on
31 December 1965.

A Bread-and-butter job. Typical of freight operation towards the end of steam on British Railways is this view (*above*) of 9F 2–10–0 No 92125 working south through Lancaster in 1967.

Victorian elegance. No steam in evidence here, but Patrick Stirling's eight-footer (*below*) epito-mises a period when size and aesthetic appeal were powerful considerations in the minds of railway officers. 'Public Relations' were not yet formalised, but the grandeur of a locomotive such as this was surely an attraction in its own right, even to those with only a mild interest in locomotives.

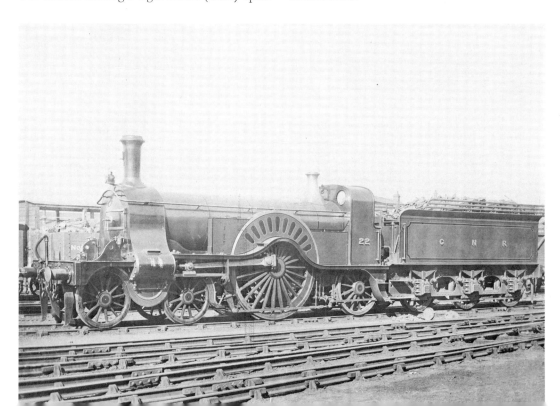

A fair amount of overlap necessarily exists amongst the conventional categories of miniature, narrow gauge and light railways. Indeed it is quite possible for a line to be all three, depending on its legal status and the kind of locomotive power possessed. Many people would no doubt reserve the term 'miniature' railway to those lines operating in parks (both private and public), pleasure-grounds, or along the sea front of a holiday resort. Yet although the Ravenglass & Eskdale or Romney, Hythe & Dymchurch companies run light railways with fairly sophisticated timetabled services over fairly long routes, the nature of their locomotives makes it convenient to consider them here as miniatures of the real thing. Gauge of itself is not theoretically decisive, though it may be remarked that no steam-operated line which really merits the epithet 'miniature' is broader than 15in.

The peculiar charm of the narrow gauge railway lies partially in its ability to arouse in the observer instincts almost paternal or maternal. The locomotives in particular remind us of children or the young of animals. They are emphatically not mere small-scale versions of the 'adult', but possess their own quite different proportions. The true miniature railway, however, evokes somewhat different responses. Photographed alone without convenient references of scale, the miniature locomotive could be mistaken for its much larger brother. One could imagine a race of Hobbits operating many a narrow gauge line; but on a miniature railway the human being, whether as driver or passenger, dominates the scene. It is a railway world where Alice has eaten too much of her magic cake or, in its smaller examples, where Gulliver has discovered the Liliputian transport system.

Ideally suited to the pleasure-ground, the miniature railway has not surprisingly gained ground in an age when noblemen have thrown their halls and parks open to the public. Operation is (unfortunately!) not invariably steam, yet even where diesel or electric power is well entrenched, the general appearance of the locomotives still celebrates the days of coal and water.

Miniature railways are unashamedly part and parcel of the entertainments industry. Their very creation is proof of the powerful hold which steam has had – and continues to have– on the public imagination.

The Ravenglass & Eskdale Railway, originally opened in 1875 as a 3ft-gauge mineral line, was acquired in 1915 by Narrow Gauge Railways Ltd. This company had been established by W. J. Bassett-Lowke and R. Proctor Mitchell in 1911 essentially to promote miniature railway operation and salvage the work of pioneers in the field. Not surprisingly the now derelict Cumberland iron-ore line seemed a golden opportunity for conversion. Regauging to 15 in began immediately, but only through the help of Sir Aubrey Brocklebank, the famous shipowner (who acquired a controlling interest in 1924), was the railway placed on a firm footing. The carriage of granite ensured that the line remained open until after the second world war. In 1948 the Keswick Granite Company bought the railway but found after a decade that it was no longer a profitable side of their business.

Fortunately it was finally bought by enthusiast interests who in 1961 established the Ravenglass & Eskdale Company Ltd. Since then this picturesque line has been fully overhauled. (*Above*) W. J. Bassett-Lowke's pioneer 15in gauge Atlantic *Little Giant* at Ravenglass with its present owner Tom Tate on the right. This locomotive was discovered by chance on a pile of scrap and then extensively restored.

(*Opposite page*) Both our photographs show one of the Ravenglass & Eskdale Railway's 2-8-2 steam locomotives, *River Mite*, at Dalegarth. Built by Clarksons of York, delivery was taken of this superb engine in December 1966. Her smart livery of Indian red, lined in black and yellow (from the Furness Railway) makes her a natural centre of admiration, here at the head of this seven mile long railway.

The very length of the Romney, Hythe &
Dymchurch Railway – 13¾ miles from Hythe to
Dungeness – would alone make it unique among
miniature lines. But for many other reasons, too,
the RH&D is quite without peer. In its standards
of engineering, layout, clever use of scale and in
the beauty of its operation, it has long been
recognised as providing steam entertainment of

the very highest quality. The brainchild of
Captain Howey and Count Louis Zborowski
(who unfortunately died before the idea was
fully realised), the line was opened in 1927 and
completed to Dungeness the following year. The
railway quickly became a favourite during
the summer months and attracted royal patronage
on several occasions. During the last war it

carried troops, thus making its own tiny contribution to the war effort. The line possesses a wealth of elegant locomotive power. The photograph (*opposite page*) captures the company's No 9, the 4–6–2 Canadian type *Winston Churchill*, on the turntable at Hythe. The driver is Mr. J. B. Snell, author and managing director of the RH&D. In the photograph (*above*) we see a typical summer-load of passengers accommodated in the company's fine rolling stock. The train, which is about to leave Hythe, is headed by 4–8–2 *Hercules* which is evidently in the very pink of mechanical condition. Certainly it is starting with a good head of steam!

Like the Ravenglass & Eskdale, the Fairbourne Railway in Merionethshire began life as a small mineral line (1890), was converted for steam operation on a 15in gauge by Narrow Gauge Railways Ltd from 1916, and was later owned for a time by Sir Aubrey Brocklebank. After the second world war the railway was rescued from virtual dereliction by a new company who bought it from Fairbourne Estates, overhauled or renewed the track and gradually added stock of every kind. It now provides Easter and Summer services over its two mile track for holiday-makers visiting the Fairbourne and Barmouth areas. (*Above*) 2–4–2 *Siân* at Fairbourne. (*Below*) the same locomotive in operation. The railway is single track with passing loops and in addition to its termini at Fairbourne and Penrhyn Point, has three small intermediate stations.

(*Above*) The Sutton Park Railway was originally opened in 1908 and enjoyed a somewhat intermittent existence until 1957.

It is shown here in its final phase with *Sutton Belle* heading a train of coaches from the Yarmouth Miniature Railway. The locomotive was built for the Hardwick Manor line by Carron Company at Dudley and was then named *Douglas* *Clayton*. It was overhauled in 1948 for the Sutton Park line.

(*Below*) The 15 in Longleat Railway was opened in 1965 and operated on the Marquess of Bath's estates by Minirail Ltd. The locomotive shown here, *Muffin*, was built by Berwyn Engineering Ltd in 1968.

Many miniature railways have been (and still are) temporary affairs – sometimes laid down in connection with a great exhibition or other important public event.

(*Opposite page*)
This $14\frac{1}{2}$in gauge railway was a great attraction at the Glasgow Exhibition of 1901. It was built by the great contemporary enthusiast, Captain Paul Boyton, over a length of 160yd and the locomotive reputedly came from Baldwins of Philadelphia. A good head of steam appears to be ready for a run whose speed might attain 12mph!

(*Above*)
At so many points of British history the public-spirited landowner has added much to the cause of conservation. Miniature railways naturally have proved to be an exciting element of any family outing to the local 'great house' and its park and gardens. The degree of commitment to the spirit of railway operation must naturally vary. But who could fault Lord Gretton's Stapleford [Park] Miniature Railway, near Melton Mowbray, opened in 1958? It runs for about a mile on a $10\frac{1}{4}$in gauge and surely its greatest pride must be the magnificent *Berkshire*, a 2–8–4 American-type locomotive actually built at Stapleford and much admired at the Model Railway Exhibition in 1972.

It was, of course, the great 'Railway Adventure' of the Talyllyn, so evocatively described by L. T. C. Rolt, that first illustrated the practicality of railway resurrection. In this case the corpse was still warm but the Festiniog Railway, the next to be tackled, needed more than the kiss of life – rather major transplant surgery. Its success was followed by revival of the Welshpool & Llanfair Railway, and then by even more ambitious projects – reconstruction of the Welsh Highland and Corris railways and construction of new lines on old trackbeds at Llanberis and Bala. The driving force behind the later schemes was the success of the first two in attracting passengers, and this new-found popularity extended to the surviving hill-climbing lines from Aberystwyth to Devil's Bridge and up Snowdon. Recently successfully promoted as the 'Great Little Trains of Wales', these railways have not only focussed attention on the attractions of the narrow-gauge, but have provided useful models for standard-gauge railway operation by amateurs. The diminutive locomotives are naturally the centre of attraction – as they were in the far-off days when the Festiniog pioneered the use of steam power on the 2ft gauge, and when the double-ended Fairlie first showed its potential. You can still ride behind a Fairlie on the Festiniog and hear it working flat-out while quaffing a pint of beer, perhaps the most civilised railway experience in Britain today! The Welsh lines, though undoubtedly the most important, are not the only steam narrow-gauge lines in Britain. Apart from miniature railways, there are the Leighton Buzzard Light Railway, the Bicton Woodland Railway, the Sittingbourne & Kemsley Light Railway and a handful of others. Each has a fascination of its own, but the real attraction on each is the 'lovable' little steam engine.

'The Daddy of them all' the Talyllyn Railway at Towyn Wharf. No one who has read L. T. C. Rolt's marvellously evocative *Railway Adventure* can be in any doubt about the central appeal of the steam locomotives in the revival of this superannuated Welsh line. The success of this project sparked off interest in railway preservation in general. The line had, however, been a tourist attraction for many years before its revival. One of the characters in Mr Rolt's story is *Edward Thomas*, built for the Corris Railway by Kerr, Stuart & Co in 1921, and bought at a generous price from British Railways in 1951. In this view the locomotive is about to leave with a train of *new* standard coaches for Abergynolwyn, its attraction obviously undimmed by time.

The Festiniog Railway earned a reputation in the 1860s for the success of its first Fairlie patent locomotive. More than a hundred years later locomotives of this type are still a feature of the line. Lacking the cosiness of the Talyllyn or the pastoral appeal of the Welshpool & Llanfair, the Festiniog is perhaps the most exciting of all British narrow-gauge railways, with its dramatic climb from sea level at Portmadoc to rugged mountain scenery at Tan-y-Bwlch and Dduallt.

The frontier image created by the new line to Blaenau Ffestiniog, at present under construction, the skilful blending of the old and new in operation and rolling stock, and the hard work demanded of the locomotives are all elements in the attraction of this splendid line. In these scenes *Little Wonder* is seen with a trial train in 1869 and its recently reboilered descendent *Merddin Emrys* shunts its train at Portmadoc Harbour station in 1971.

Resembling the Festiniog in the steepness of its ascent of the Rheidol valley, the line from Aberystwyth to Devil's Bridge has several unique features. It is owned by British Rail and has the only steam locomotives operated by that organisation. When built in the early years of this century it had such refinements as gas lighting at the main stations, but it is now very much a 'basic railway'. Tourist traffic was expected by its promoters, and has been the mainstay of the line throughout its existence. The chunky Great Western Railway – built 2–6–2Ts have a thoroughly professional air about them and this is confirmed by their work on the climb up the valley. Here *Owain Glyndŵr* is seen at Aberystwyth station (the former Manchester & Milford Railway platforms, converted to narrow gauge in 1968) and at Devil's Bridge terminus.

Almost exactly contemporary with the Vale of Rheidol line, but very different in character, is the Welshpool & Llanfair Railway. It, too, became part of British Rail, and with its Great Westernised locomotives looked like a scaled down version of 'God's Wonderful Railway'. Since reopened by a preservation company in 1963 the concern has acquired a thoroughly cosmopolitan appearance, with coaches from the Zillertalbahn and the Salzkammergut Lokalbahn and an o-8-oT from the latter line. The Austrian coaches feature (*above*), with one from the Chattenden & Upnor Light Railway (immediately behind the locomotive). The train is headed by *The Countess*, one of the two original engines, and is about to leave Castle Caereinion for Llanfair Caereinion.

(*Above, opposite page*)
The extraordinary success of the Welsh narrow-gauge railways, has resulted in two new creations, the Llanberis Lake Railway and the Bala Lake Railway, both on the formation of abandoned lines. These are specifically commercial ventures, and they use the economical 2ft gauge. Here *Dolbadarn*, formerly of the Padarn Railway, runs round its train at the temporary Cei Llydan

terminus on the locally financed Llanberis Lake line. *Dolbadarn*, built in 1922, is one of the standard Hunslet o-4-o saddle tanks used in the Dinorwic Quarries, while the route of the railway is over part of the 4ft gauge line from the quarries to Port Dinorwic, abandoned in 1962.

(*Below, opposite page*)
Perhaps the most elegant of recently surviving narrow-gauge lines in the British Isles is the Isle of Man Railway, which operated commercially until 1965. Latterly the winter trains were diesel railcars, but steam came into its own for summer traffic, which was very heavy indeed. The island is too distant from the mainland for regular volunteer operation, so it was very welcome when the railway was revived, first by a private company, and more recently by a Manx Government subsidy. Thus it is that the graceful little Beyer-Peacock 2-4-oTs may still be seen running from the splendid Douglas terminus to Port Erin, at the south end of the island. In this view, taken in 1964, *Fenella* of 1894 and *Mona* of 1874 are seen with a good head of steam at Douglas waiting to take trains to Peel and Ramsey.

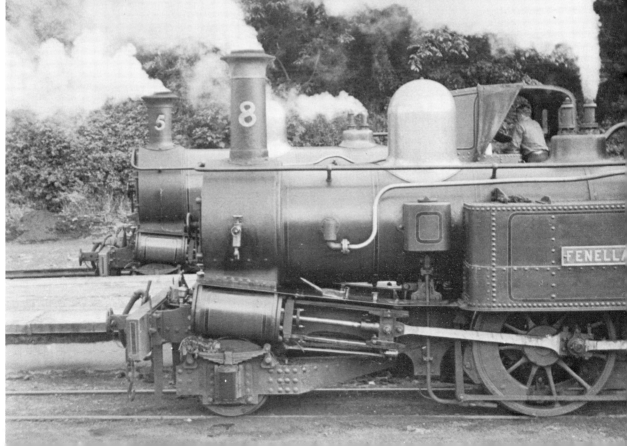

Unusual among the narrow-gauge enthusiast-operated lines is the 2ft gauge Leighton Buzzard Light Railway industrial line which for most of its life used internal-combustion-engined locomotives. Here *Chaloner*, a de Winton slate quarry locomotive of 1877, is getting steam up for a train.

In this view *Pixie* a Kerr Stuart Wren class
0–4–0ST built in 1922 is seen descending
Marley's Bank on the Leighton Buzzard Light
Railway.

(*Above*)
Perhaps the most remarkable locomotive on the Leighton Buzzard Light Railway is *Rishra*, a Baguley 0–4–0T of 1921 discovered acting as a clothes post near Calcutta and shipped back in 1971. Here she is crossing the Clipstone Brook by 'Swing Swang' bridge.

(*Left*) *Pixie* approaching Slanbridge Road during firemen's examinations.

(*Above, opposite page*)
A Snowdon Mountain railway train with locomotive No 5, *Moel Siabod*, in July 1967. The Snowdon line is the only steam-worked mountain railway in the British Isles, and has affinities with comparable continental lines – including Swiss built locomotives.

(*Below, opposite page*)
No 2, *Enid* at Llanberis, with weather protection clearly evident.

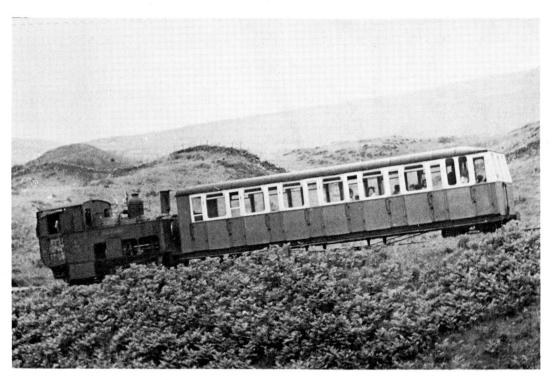

Industrial lines have indeed been a prolific source of locomotives for narrow-gauge pleasure lines. Here are two more: *No 1*, from the Padarn Railway, with toastrack coaches is at Knebworth House, while *Conqueror*, from Bowater's railway at Sittingbourne is seen on the Whipsnade & Umfolozi Railway, from which passengers can safely view the herd of white rhinoceros at Whipsnade Zoo. In both cases the gauge suits the locomotive – 2ft at Knebworth and 2ft 6in at Whipsnade.

Both lines were built and are operated by Pleasurerail Ltd, an enterprise curiously similar in spirit to the pioneering Miniature Railways of Great Britain Ltd formed by W. J. Bassett-Lowke in 1904.

Bord na Mona was never like this! A scene on The Lord O'Neill's Shane's Castle Railway in Ireland, with one of three steam locomotives built by Andrew Barclay, Sons & Co Ltd, Kilmarnock, in 1949 for the Irish Turf Board. (The other two are also 'preserved'; one will eventually become *Irish Pete* on the Talyllyn Railway.)

This railway is built to a gauge of 3ft, and in its function as a tourist attraction resembles some of the miniature railways described in section 4.

On the Shane's Castle Railway, No 3 at speed in a sylvan setting and (opposite) approaching a level crossing.

Smaller in gauge, but similar in spirit, are Alan Bloom's 2ft gauge lines at his Bressingham Steam Museum, Diss, Norfolk. Mr Bloom has charmingly described the genesis of these lines in *Steam Engines at Bressingham*. (*Above*) a train on the Nursery Railway is headed by Orenstein & Koppel 0–4–0WT *Eigiau* of 1912, formerly of the Penrhyn Quarry railway, North Wales.

(*Above, opposite page*)
The gauge of the charming Lincolnshire Coast Light Railway is 2ft and the line can trace its commercial origins back to the era of small agricultural railways related chiefly to the county's heavy potato production. Enthusiast intervention began in the 1950s and by August 1960 the company was able to open with diesel locomotion. We show steam of course! *Jurassic*,

a Peckett 0–6–0ST is seen leaving North Sea Lane station, Humberston, Grimsby. The mile-long line has proved extremely popular with holiday makers to Cleethorpes.

(*Below, opposite page*)
The only direct conversion from narrow gauge industrial railway to pleasure line in Britain is the Sittingbourne & Kemsley Light Railway, product of a fruitful collaboration between paper giant Bowater, (which owns the line, and kept it in full steam operation until 1968), and the Locomotive Club of Great Britain. Here in unashamedly industrial surroundings green locomotives and red and white coaches provide a sparkle of colour. In this spring 1972 scene Bagnall 0–6–2T *Superb* is at Sittingbourne with a train from Kemsley.

Standard gauge railway, as opposed to locomotive, preservation in Britain started with the reopening of the Bluebell Railway in 1960, but earlier the main line railways, realising the appeal of vintage steam, had in a few instances brought old timers back into service. The railway centenary celebration on the Stockton & Darlington Railway in 1925 was the grandest of these occasions, with some of the oldest locomotives in the world on view to an enormous audience. The LNER followed this in 1938 by operating GNR Stirling eight-footer No 1 on excursions. The war and subsequent austerity put a stop to such jollifications, and survivors of obsolete types languished in museums. It was the impending end of steam traction on British Railways that brought about an indian summer when museum-pieces were extracted and overhauled, and examples of famous classes still in service were restored to original liveries. Before this period had ended some railway enthusiasts had taken the bold step of reviving standard-gauge lines. The success of the Bluebell Railway was at first isolated, but in the late 1960s the Dart Valley, Keighley & Worth Valley and Severn Valley schemes came to fruition. Unusual projects included the Middleton Railway Trust, which still operates freight services all the year round, and the Lochty Private Railway Company, surely the only railway ever to operate with a total locomotive stock of one Pacific. At the time of writing this new 'railway mania' is still in full swing, with new lines in all stages of projection, from mere proposals to virtual completion, as in the cases of the North York Moors and Kent & East Sussex railways. Apart from such *railway* preservation schemes, locomotive preservation has become popular, and with income inflation more rapid than the rise in the price of scrap, more and more individuals or small groups can afford to buy locomotives. Many industrial locomotives have been presented for preservation by both private firms and public corporations. There can be no more convincing argument for the entertainment value of steam locomotives than the amount of time, money and energy cheerfully spent on their voluntary preservation and operation.

The Bluebell Railway was the first enthusiast-operated standard-gauge line in Britain, and retains the flavour of the southern English branch line very effectively. In the early days of operation on this railway, absence of run-round facilities meant that trains had to have an engine at each end, and here a train is seen at Sheffield Park, the line's headquarters, with no fewer than four locomotives, ex South Eastern & Chatham P class engines *Primrose* and *Bluebell*, ex-London, Brighton & South Coast Railway Terrier class *Stepney* and an ex-London & South Western Railway Adams 4–4–2T No 488.

Here the Bluebell Railway train illustrated on the previous page is seen from the other end, with the P class engines *Bluebell* and *Primrose* in evidence.

One does not need to be a rabid railway enthus- Here is North Eastern Railway class P3 No 2392
iast to enjoy a day out on the North Yorkshire at Grosmont Station.
Moors Railway in a remote and beautiful setting.

(*Opposite page*)
In these views on the North Yorkshire Moors line family groups inspect locomotives at Goathland on a weekday. As with many other preservation schemes, industrial locomotives are in a majority, and here we see *Mirvale* a Hudswell Clarke product of 1955 and a rather larger 0–4–0ST by Hawthorn Leslie.

(*Right*)
It's never too early to start. Schoolchildren dismounting from WD150, a Hunslet Austerity 0–6–0ST at Dinting Railway Centre, with a Barclay 0–4–0ST in the background. WD150 is fitted with an underfeed stoker to reduce smoke emission.

(*Below*)
Children wait for *Nunlow* (left) or WD150.

Behind the scenes. Preservation of steam locomotives in working order is not easy, and their
maintenance often requires considerable agility.
In this view of Manning Wardle 0–6–0ST *Sir*
Berkeley at Haworth on the Keighley & Worth
Valley Railway, one enthusiast is obviously
cleaning up externally. Less conspicuously, a
pair of feet protrude below the smokebox.

Steam in Scotland. A Barclay 0–4–0ST attracts attention as it heads a train of ex LMS coaches at a Scottish Railway Preservation Society open day in Stirling in April 1972.

(*Above*)
Perhaps the most famous of all preserved steam locomotives (as it is surely the most romantic) is the *Flying Scotsman*. It is seen here at Newcastle-upon-Tyne before its somewhat unfortunate visit to America.

(*Below*)
The end of the line. Gresley A4 No 60009 *Union of South Africa* at Knightsward terminus on the privately owned Lochty Railway in Fife in 1971 with a train consisting of an ex BR standard coach and one of the former Coronation beaver tail observation cars.
This locomotive returned to BR metals in 1973 for special excursions.

On the marches. The Severn Valley Railway with one of the most extensive collections of equipment of any of the standard-gauge operating lines, representing both LMS and GWR interests, successfully recaptures the atmospheres, not of a branch line, but of a secondary cross-country line. Here Stanier class 5 No 45110 raises the echoes at Bridgnorth with LMS stock. The pleasantly wooded landscape through which the line passes is clearly seen here.

The Severn Valley Railway in contrasting
moods.

(Above)
Ivatt 2–6–0 No 46443 in wintry weather at
Eardington.

(Opposite page)
Collett 0–6–0 No 3205 leaving Bridgnorth in
high summer with a train of GWR stock.

(*Opposite page, above*) Class 5 4–6–0 No 5025 is the centre of attraction at Keighley Station on the Keighley & Worth Valley Railway. Rescued from the scrap road by Mr W. E. C. Watkinson, Honorary President of the Scottish Railway Preservation Society, overhauled by the Hunslet Engine Company Ltd in Leeds, and restored to its original LMS livery, 5025 has been on loan to the K&WVR pending transfer to the Aviemore – Boat of Garten line. (*Opposite page, below*) A Lady's engine: this Ivatt 2–6–0 at Steamtown, Carnforth, belongs to Mrs Peter Beet, and has been repainted in a most attractive, if unprototypical, version of LMS livery. Probably the best-equipped of the depot preservation schemes, Steamtown houses a wide variety of locomotives, including a French Pacific. Here one can capture at least some of the flavour of a working main-line steam running shed.

(*Above*)

The Dart Valley Railway is unique among standard-gauge preserved lines it that it adheres to the practice of a single main-line company – the Great Western – and in its emphasis on commercial viability. It has proved one of the most successful railway preservation ventures, and the acquisition of the Paignton–Kingswear line in 1973 as a second string has proved an attraction to Torbay holiday makers. No 4555, a Churchward 2–6–2T, is seen on a train which includes the former Devon Belle observation car in its make-up, at Buckfastleigh.

The professional railwayman's love of the steam locomotive was never more openly displayed than in a short period in the late 1950s and early 1960s when museum pieces steamed again. On the Western Region, *City of Truro* led the way, but it was on the Scottish Region under Mr James Ness that large-scale revival took place, with the restoration of Caledonian Railway 4–2–2 No 123 and Highland Railway 4–6–0 No 103 to working order and the refurbishing of Great North of Scotland Railway *Gordon Highlander* and North British Railway *Glen Douglas*, both 4–4–0s. Together with *City of Truro*, brought up to Scotland for the occasion, this quartet ran

special trains in connection with the Scottish Industries Exhibition of 1959, and they continued to haul enthusiast specials for some years thereafter. In 1966 except for *City of Truro* which went to Swindon they were moved into the Glasgow Museum of Transport. (*Above, opposite page*) No 123 is seen at Stirling in 1964 on a Stephenson Locomotive Society special to Callander. (*Below, opposite page*) *Gordon Highlander* approaches Eglinton Street Station on another SLS special in 1965. (*Above*) No 103 stands at Inverness in 1956 with a Highland Railway Centenary Special.

The torch lit by James Ness in 1957, when he had No 123 put into working order, has been carried on by the Scottish Railway Preservation Society, which owns the only Scottish main-line locomotive at present operable, Caledonian Railway 0-4-4T No 419 of 1907. Here 419 storms up a gradient in Springfield Yard, Falkirk with a one-coach train at an open day in September 1972.

(*Above*)

How many children can get on a pug? Enjoyment rather than education seems to be the order of the day in this view of the South of Scotland Electricity Board's Yoker Power Station shunter. The occasion – an open weekend held for Clyde International '72 at Rothesay Dock, Clydebank by the Scottish Railway Preservation Society. The 'pug' (Scots for a small tank engine) was repainted in light blue, yellow, black and red for the event.

(*Below*)

Changed days, when footplate trips can be justified as education. Here Lancashire schoolchildren are evidently enjoying a ride on *Nunlow* at the Dinting Railway Centre, Glossop, on the occasion of a special schools open day in June 1972. *Nunlow*, an industrial 0–6–0 side tank built by Hudswell Clarke in 1938, has been most beautifully painted in Great Central Railway green.

The Castles and Kings of the Great Western Railway were among the first types to attract the attention of preservationists. In these views *Clun Castle* rests at Carlisle Kingmoor after hauling an excursion.

King George V, beautifully restored under the auspices of H. P. Bulmer and Co Ltd, leaves the Severn Tunnel on the first official 'return to steam' run in England on 3 October 1971. The Pullman cars in the King's train are Bulmer-owned.

Steam in the Nursery. The rise to fame of Alan Bloom's Bressingham Museum has been quite dramatic. Beginning with traction engines, Mr Bloom has widened his practical interest in steam to include some of the largest locomotives.

Two of the most recently restored ones are seen here. LMS 4–6–0 No 6100 *Royal Scot* came from Butlin's holiday camp at Skegness, and 2500, the first Stanier three-cylinder 2–6–4T, is on loan from the British Railways Board Collection.

Acknowledgements

We wish to tender our sincere thanks to those who have allowed us to reproduce photographic material. Our particular debts are as follows: James Hall (photographers) Ltd., Greenock, page 11; T. and R. Annan (photographers), Glasgow, pages 12 and 13; Morrison and MacDonald (Paisley) Ltd., 14; Oxford City Libraries, 16 and 17; B. E. Hillsdon, Ashford, Middlesex, 18 and 19; Nottingham Historical Film Unit, 20; Clarke-Chapman John Thompson Ltd., 21 upper; National Maritime Museum, 23 lower, 24; A. E. Dandridge, Oxford, 28, 29 and 36 upper; J. A. Smith, Robberttown, Yorkshire, 30, 31 upper, 32 lower, 33; Leeds and District Traction Engine Club, 31 lower, 32 upper, 34, 36 lower, 37; His Grace the Duke of Bedford and Owen Barnes (photographers), Busby Heath, 35; Trevor Rees, Cambuslang, 41 upper, 43, 44, 47, 67, 77, 82 upper, 92, 93; Jonathan Wright, Thame, 64; James Buck, 65 lower; C. Leah, 65 upper; Pleasurerail, 68; The Lord O'Neill, 67, 70, 71; Bressingham Steam Museum, Diss, 72 and 95; J. R. Smith, 73 upper; Robin Butterell, 50 and 55 upper; M. Pope, Ealing, 52 and 53; The Reverend A. Newman, Bradford-on-Avon, 55 lower; Lord Gretton of Stapleford Park, 57; Graham E. Langmuir, Glasgow, 56; W. S. Sellar, Polmont, 75 and 76; D. C. Williams, 83, 84 and 85; R. O. Coffin, Bristol, 94.

In addition we owe debts of gratitude to Bertram Unné of Harrogate for the picture on the jacket; Dr. A. Miller of Clydebank; the Leighton Buzzard Narrow Gauge Railway Society; the Lincolnshire Coast Light Railway; Newby Hall Estates; the Romney, Hythe & Dymchurch Railway; and to the Severn Valley Railway Company Ltd. Finally we wish to thank the Marquess of Bath, and Pamela Goodger, Public Relations Officer at Longleat; H. Grayshom Lumby; C. R. Iliffe; James Ferguson (Scott-Lithgow (1969) Ltd); David Vaisey of the Bodleian Library, Oxford; Michael S. Moss and others too numerous to mention who gave us their encouragement.